Redstone and Transportation in Minecraft

By Josh Gregory

Published in the United States of America by
Cherry Lake Publishing
Ann Arbor, Michigan
www.cherrylakepublishing.com

Reading Adviser: Marla Conn, Read With Me Now
Photo Credits: Images by Josh Gregory

Library of Congress Cataloging-in-Publication Data has been filed and is available
at catalog.loc.gov

Cherry Lake Publishing would like to acknowledge the work of the Partnership for
21st Century Learning. Please visit *www.p21.org* for more information.

Printed in the United States of America
Corporate Graphics

Table of Contents

Now matter how much you play, there are always new building techniques to learn in *Minecraft*.

Bring Your Creations to Life

You've probably built all kinds of things if you've played *Minecraft* before. Have you dug underground tunnels? Maybe you've stacked stones into huge castles and towers. But did you know you can build things that move? You can also make things light up, explode, and more!

You can use Redstone to build lights that switch on and off.

A Powerful Material

The world of *Minecraft* is powered by a material called Redstone. Redstone is a lot like electricity. It can make lights turn on and off. It can make things start moving when you flip a switch. You can use it to build machines, bombs, and other amazing devices.

Minecraft 1.8.8

Blocks of Redstone look like this.

Gathering Redstone

Redstone is a lot like the other building and **crafting** materials in *Minecraft*. You can find it around the world by **mining** and exploring. Redstone looks like a gray block with red dots all over it. You'll need a pickax to destroy Redstone blocks. Each one you destroy will drop four or five pieces of Redstone dust.

No Mining Necessary

There are other ways to get Redstone. You can trade emeralds to villagers. You can also fight witches. Each witch drops up to six pieces of Redstone dust when it dies. Another easy way to get Redstone is to simply find it in treasure chests.

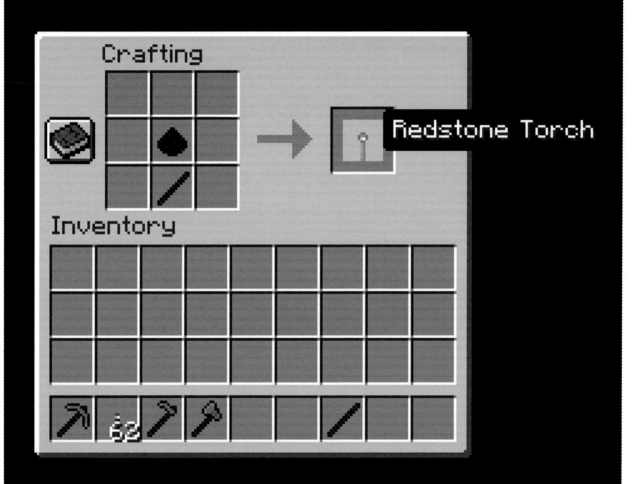

To create a Redstone torch, simply place one piece of Redstone dust on top of one stick.

Dust, Blocks, and Torches

You can lay Redstone dust down in lines to build **circuits**. Each circuit needs a power source. One possible power source is a Redstone block. You can also combine nine pieces of dust to create a solid block of Redstone. A Redstone torch is another possible power source. Combine Redstone dust with a stick to create one.

Rails are a great way to quickly travel up and down hills.

On the Move

One of the best uses of Redstone in *Minecraft* is to build railroad tracks. The world of *Minecraft* is huge. You can use rails to connect the places you travel to most often. Then you can drop a mine cart on the rails. Redstone-powered rails will send your cart zooming across the world. You'll get where you want to go much faster than by walking!

The crafting recipe for rails looks like this.

Cart Crafting

You can find regular rails and mine carts around the world of *Minecraft*. You can also craft them yourself. A cart is made from five iron **ingots**. Craft rails by combining six iron ingots and one stick. You will get 16 pieces of regular rail track.

Redstone Recipes

You can use Redstone dust to craft all kinds of useful items. Combine it with four gold ingots to make a clock. Combine it with four iron ingots to craft a **compass**.

Powered rails need a Redstone power source to work. Place a Redstone torch or Redstone block next to each one.

Laying Down Tracks

You'll also want some Redstone-powered rails. Combine six gold ingots, one stick, and one piece of Redstone dust to get six powered rails. Now build a railroad track. Most of it should be made of regular rails. Place a powered rail in between every few pieces of regular rail.

Simply set your mine cart on the rail to get started.

Riding the Rails

Place solid blocks of stone or another material at each end of your track. This will stop the cart when it reaches the end. Are you ready to ride? Set a cart down in front of a powered rail. Now get in. Press forward to move the cart onto the powered rail. The cart should start speeding up on its own!

What kinds of crazy rails will you create? Try making your own roller coaster!

Get Creative!

Now you know the basics of using Redstone. What will you build next? You can add switches and other controls to your railroad. Or you can build something entirely different. Players have used it to put automatic sliding doors in their buildings. They have also used it to create huge bombs. Can you figure out how?

Ideas Everywhere

Do you need ideas for new things to build with Redstone? Look online to see what other players have built. Their creations could help you think up amazing new projects to try on your own.

Glossary

circuits (SUR-kits) pathways for energy to travel along

compass (KUHM-puhs) a device with a magnetic pointer that always points north, used for finding directions

crafting (KRAFT-ing) making or creating

ingots (ING-guhts) masses of metal shaped into blocks or bars

mining (MYE-ning) the process of digging up resources from the ground

Find Out More

Books

Jelley, Craig. *Minecraft: Guide to Redstone*. New York: Del Rey, 2017.

Milton, Stephanie. *Minecraft Essential Handbook*. New York: Scholastic, 2015.

Milton, Stephanie. *Minecraft: Guide to Exploration*. New York: Del Rey, 2017.

Web Sites

Minecraft

https://minecraft.net/en
At the official *Minecraft* Web site, you can learn more about the game or download a copy of the PC version.

Minecraft Wiki

https://minecraft.gamepedia.com/Minecraft_Wiki
Minecraft's many fans work together to maintain this detailed guide to the game.

Index

About the Author

Josh Gregory is the author of more than 125 books for kids. He has written about everything from animals to technology to history. A graduate of the University of Missouri–Columbia, he currently lives in Chicago, Illinois.